Mandalas

Relaxing Patterns

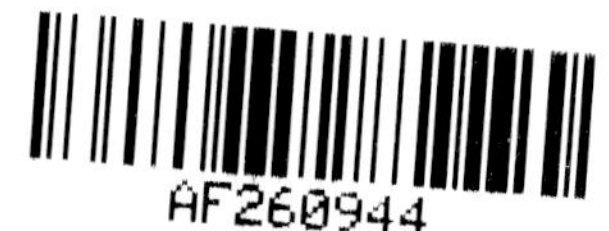

Leanne Alyse

Color Test Page

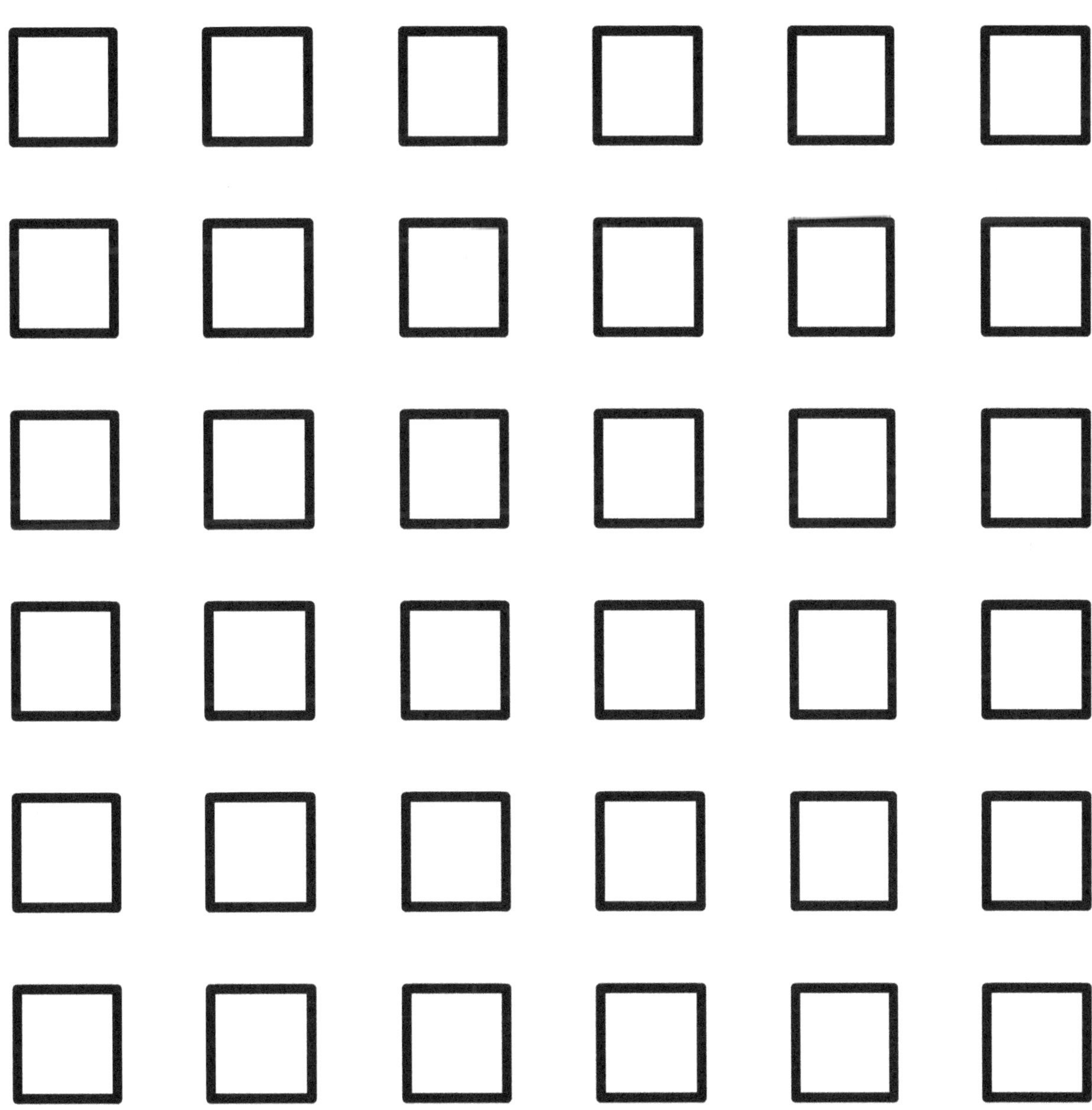

Color Test Page

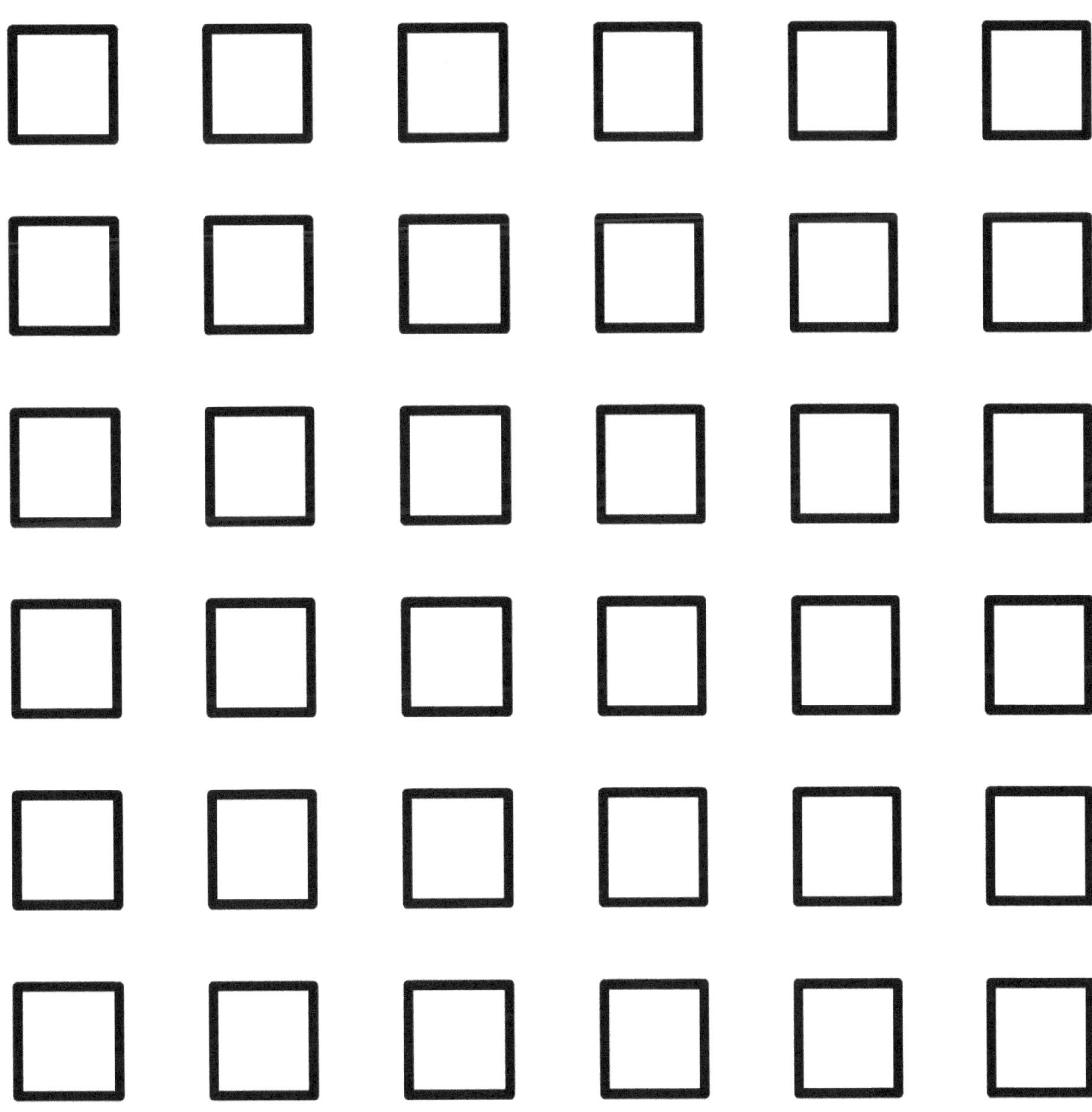

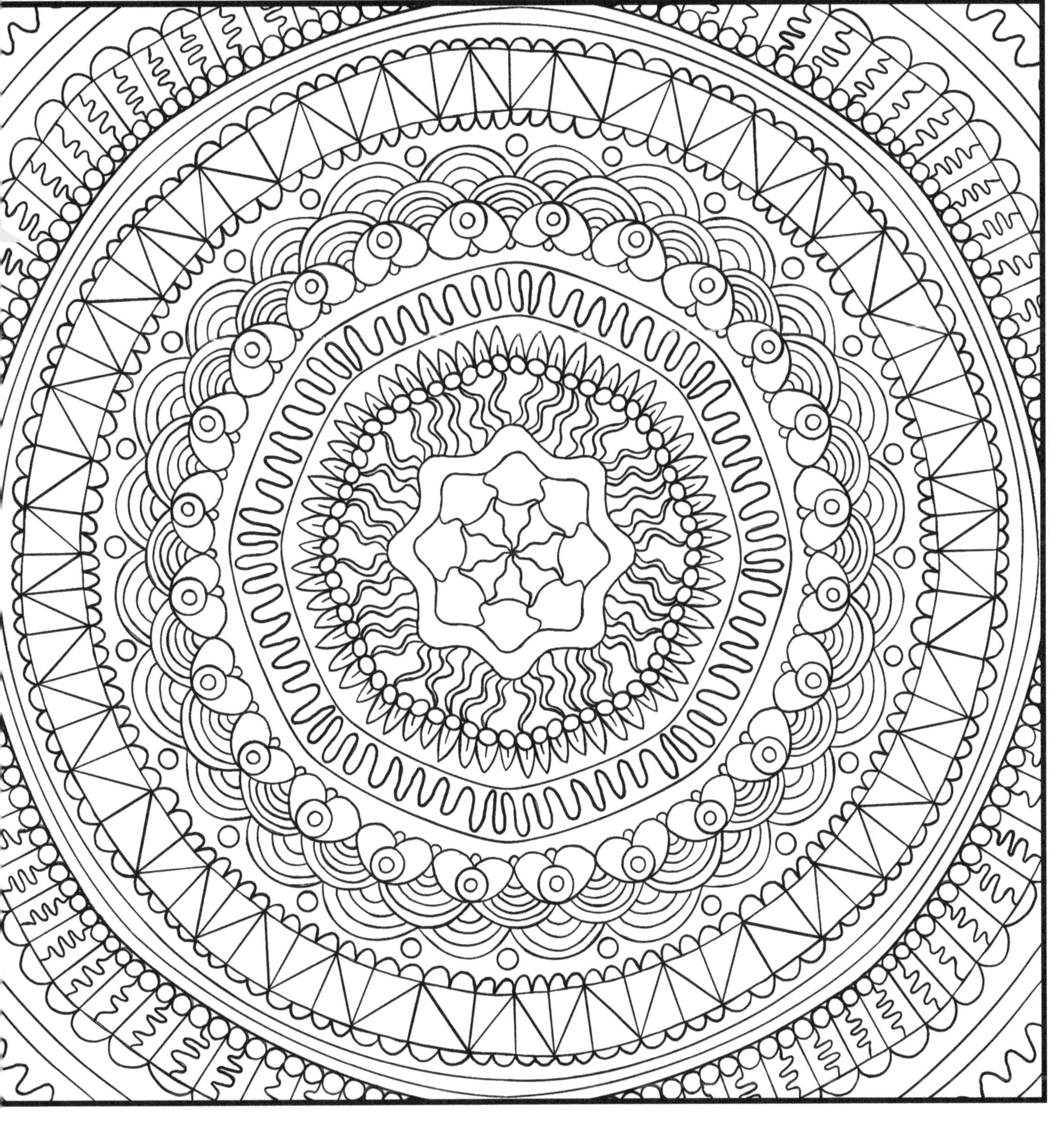

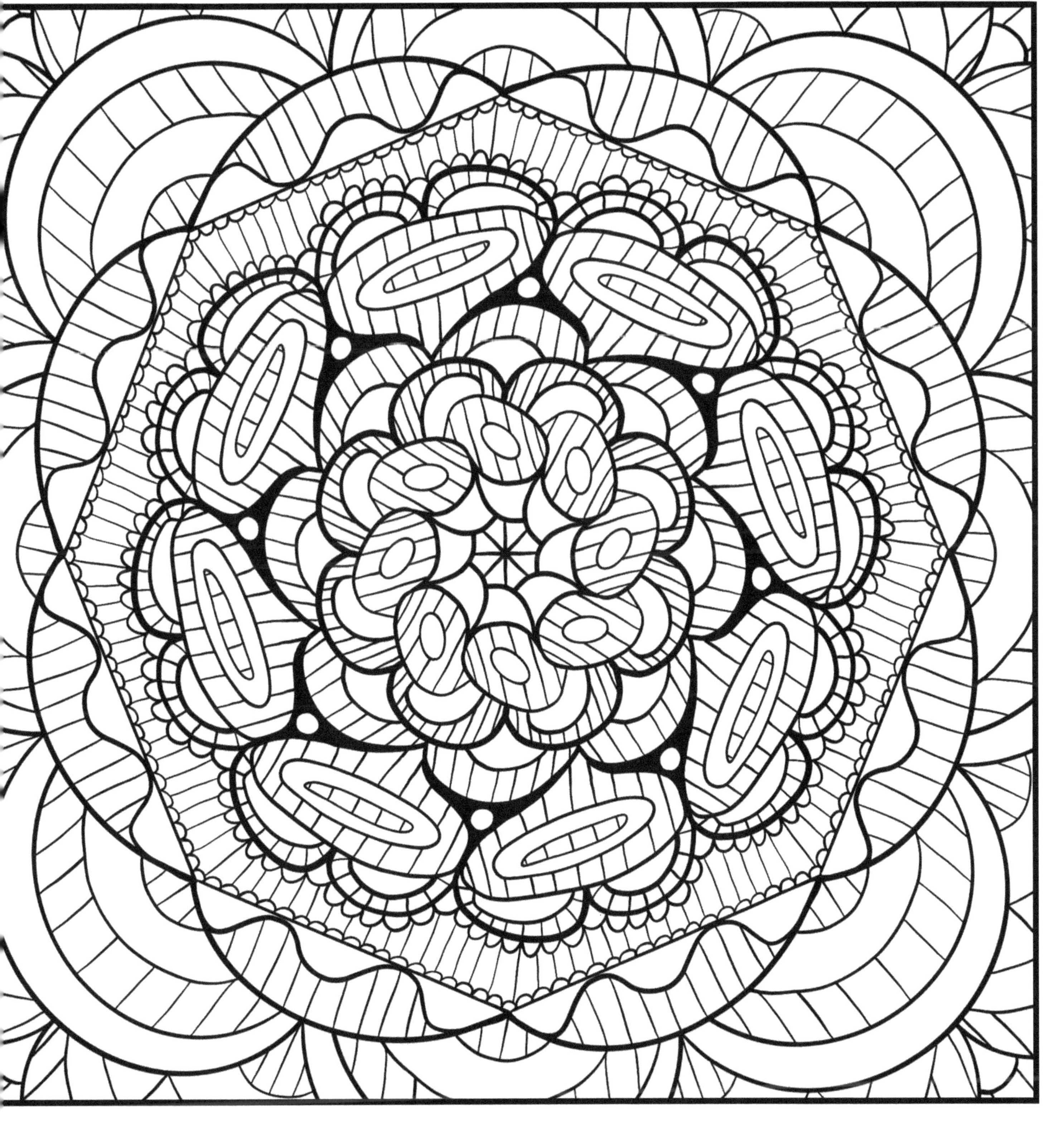

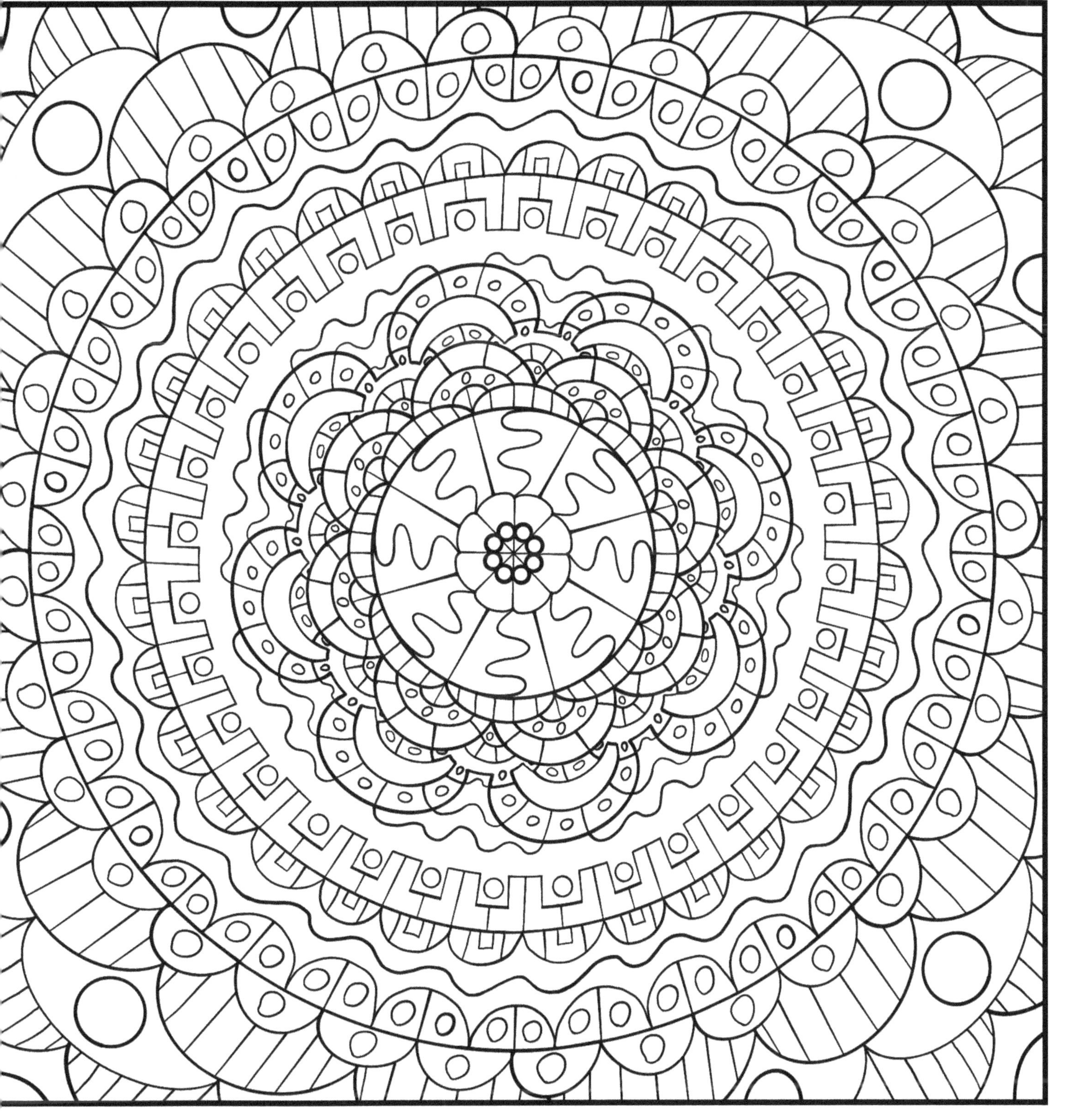

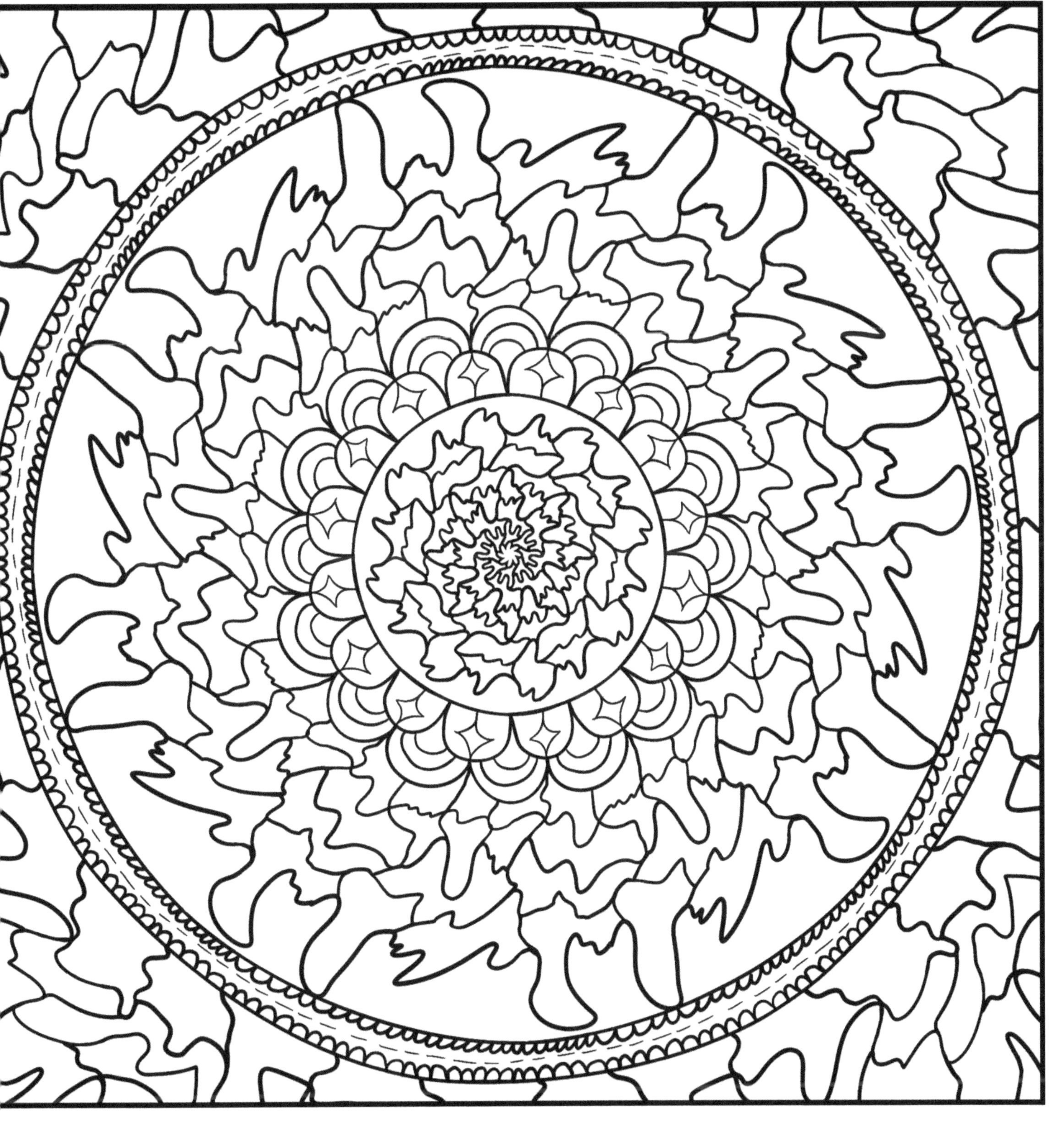

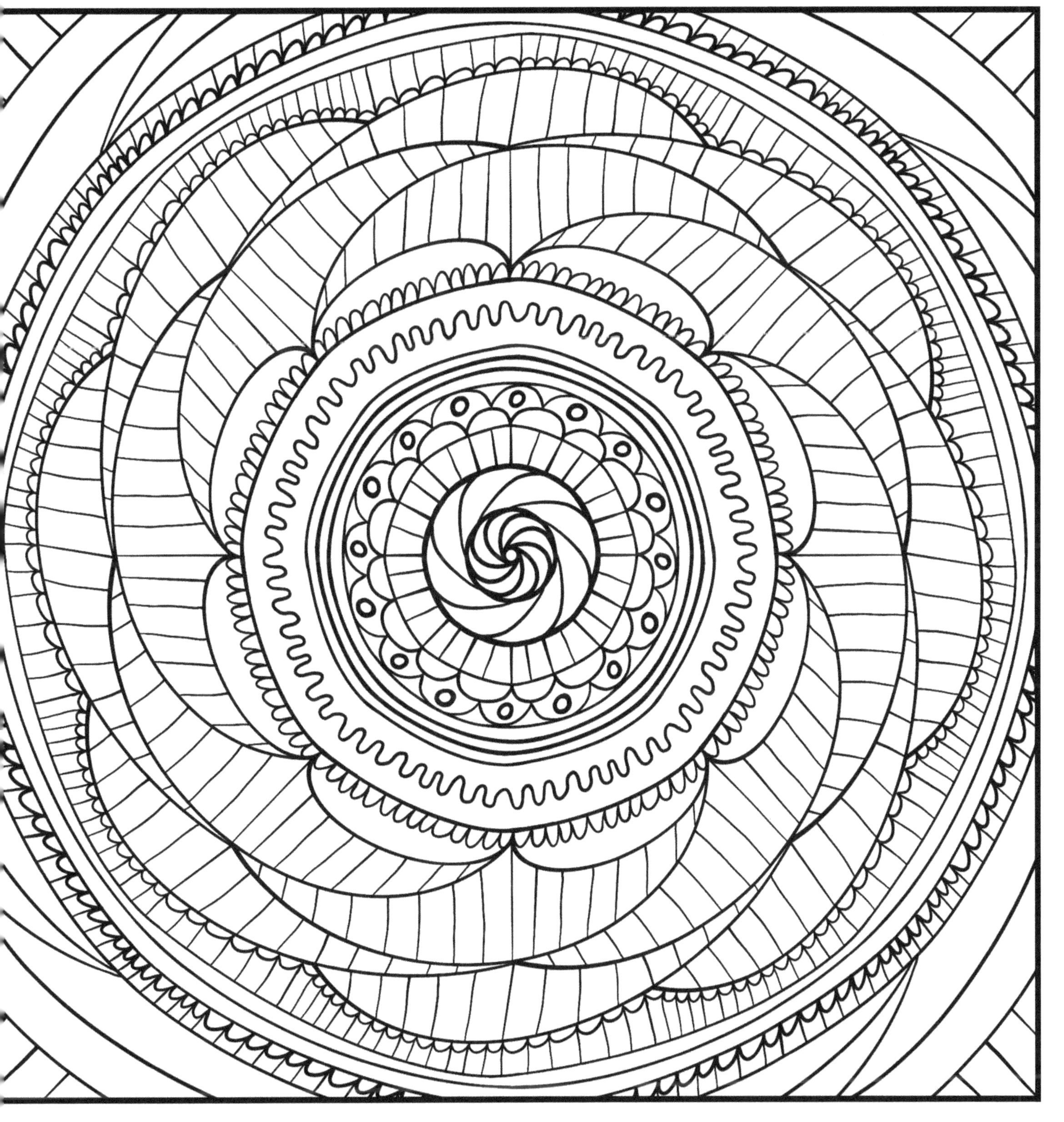

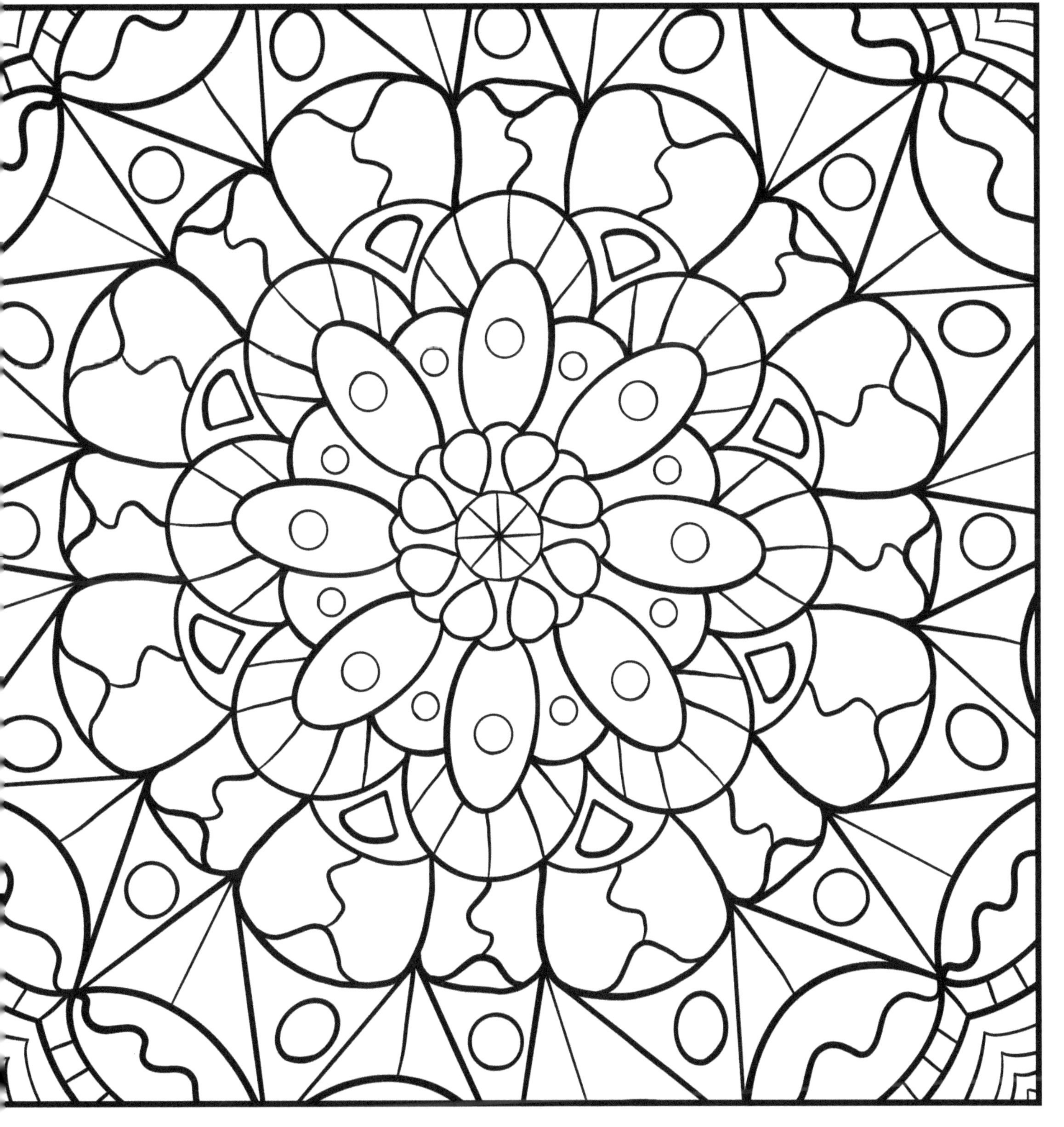

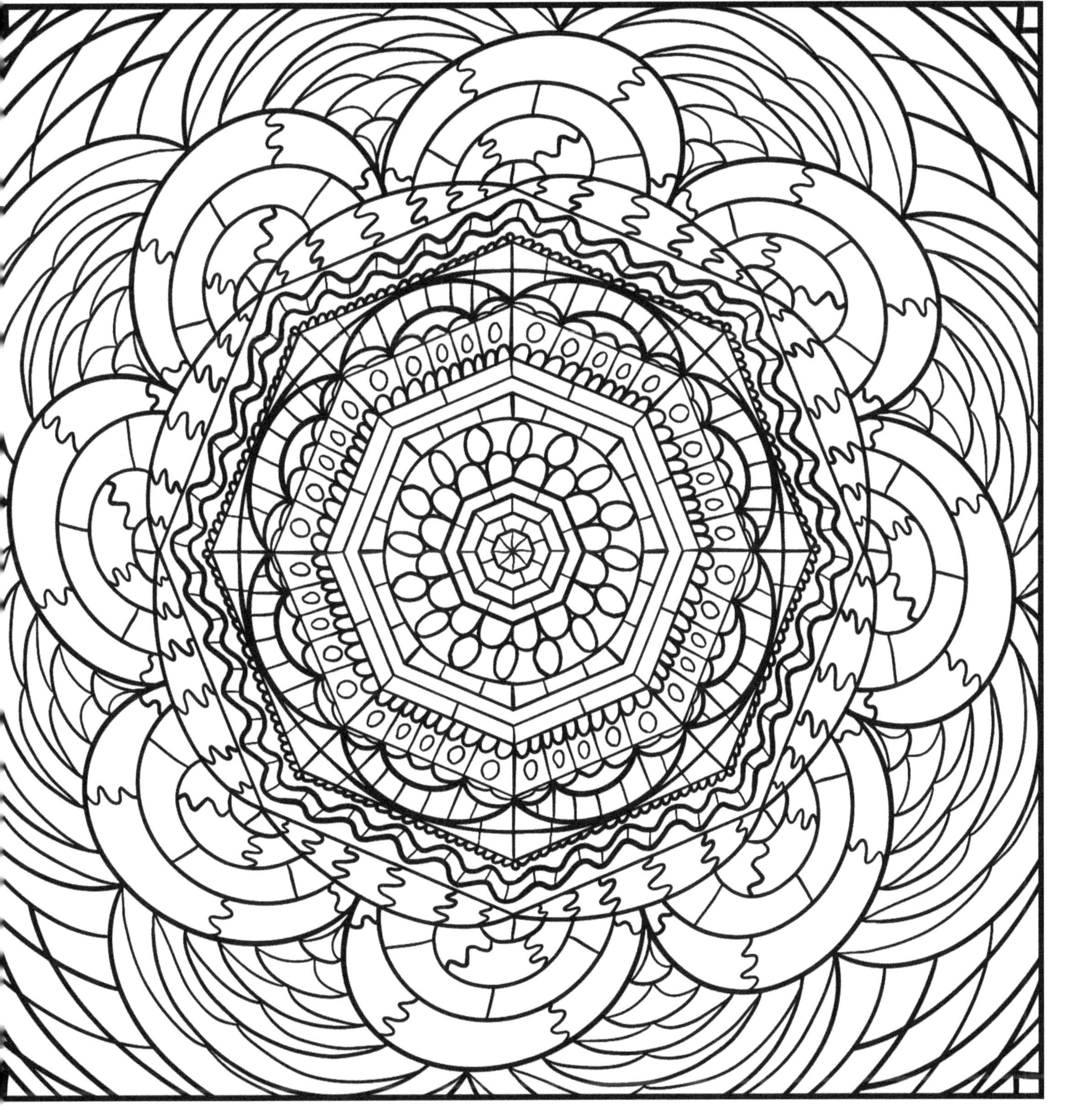

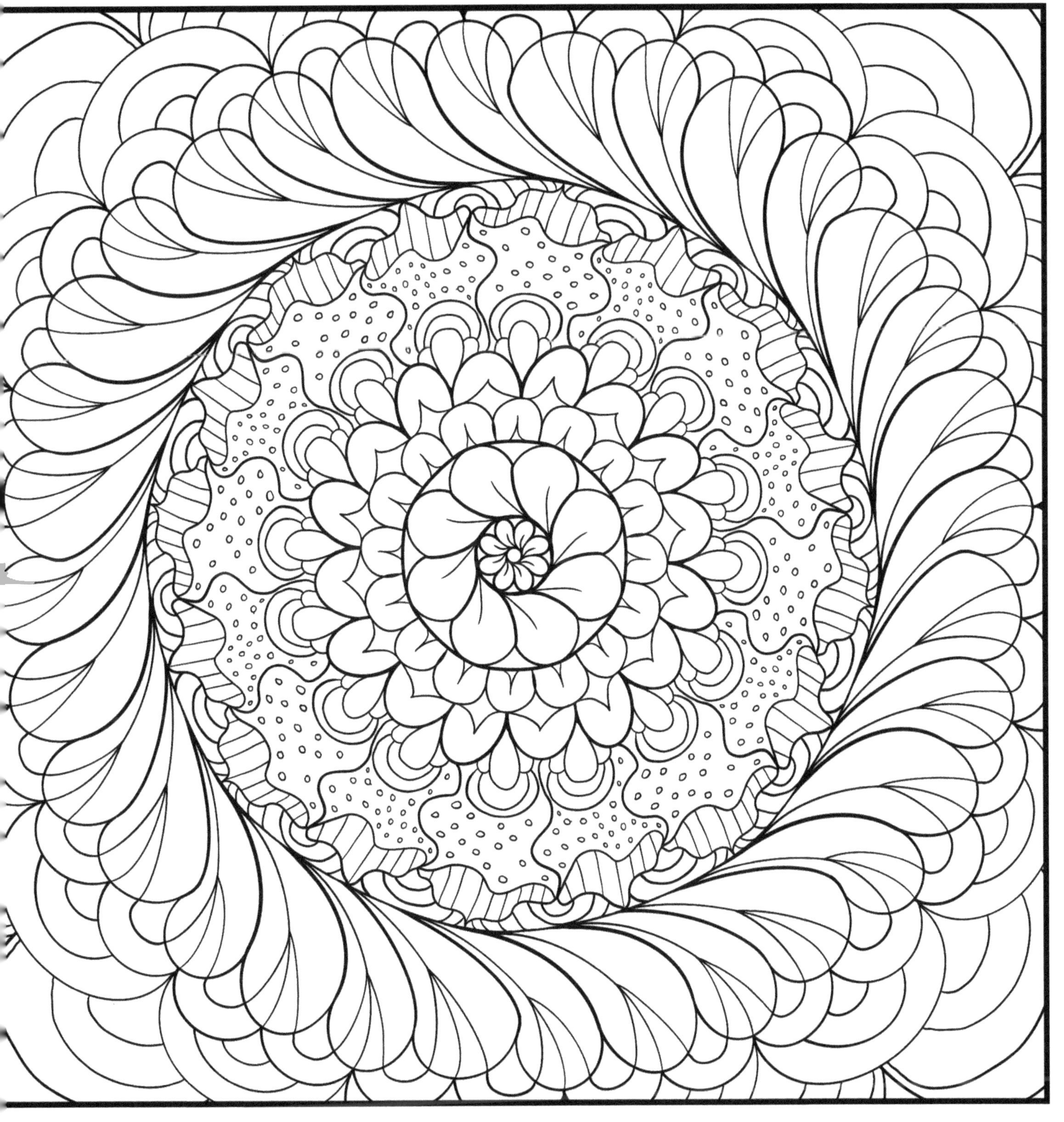

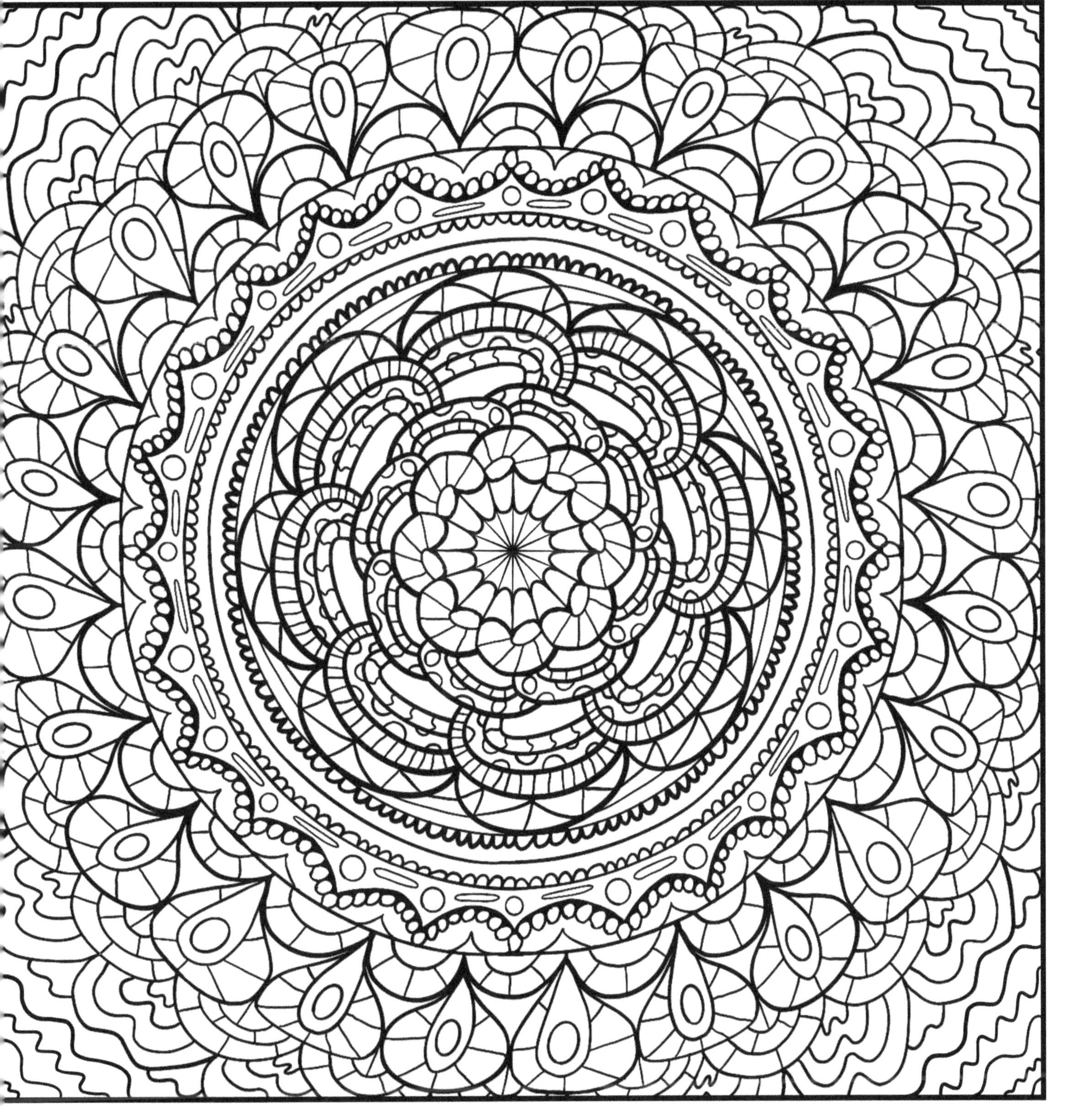

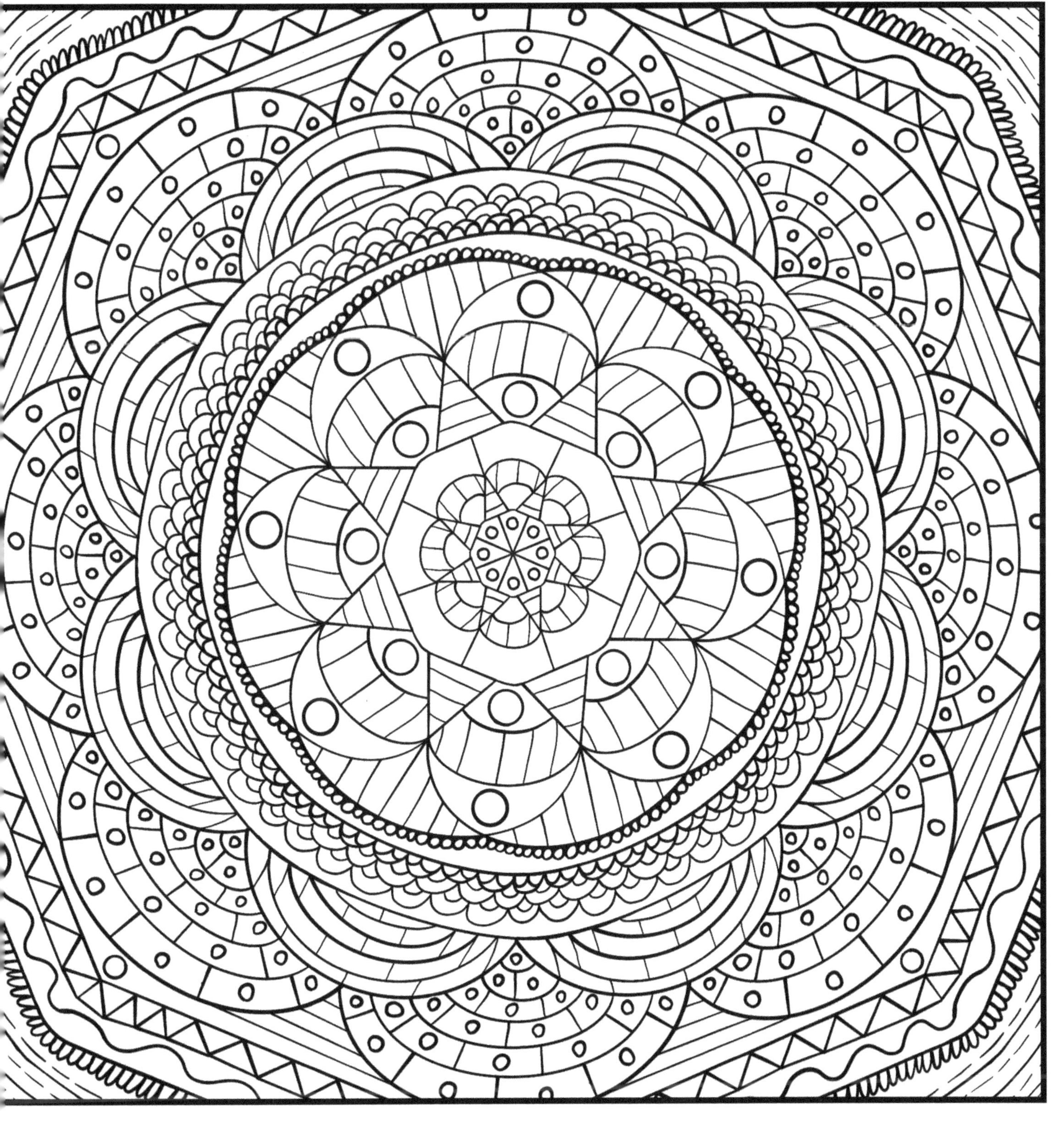

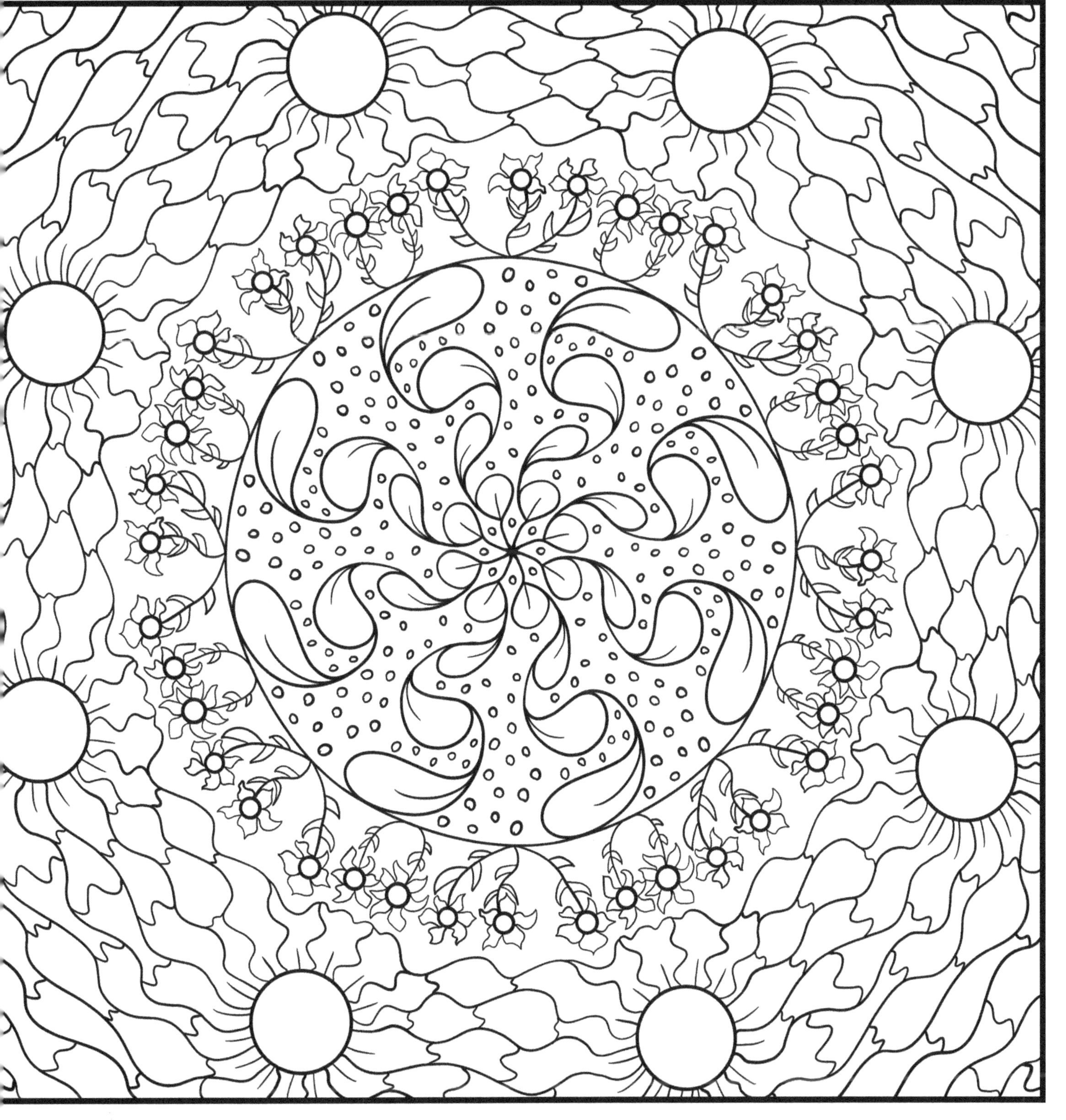

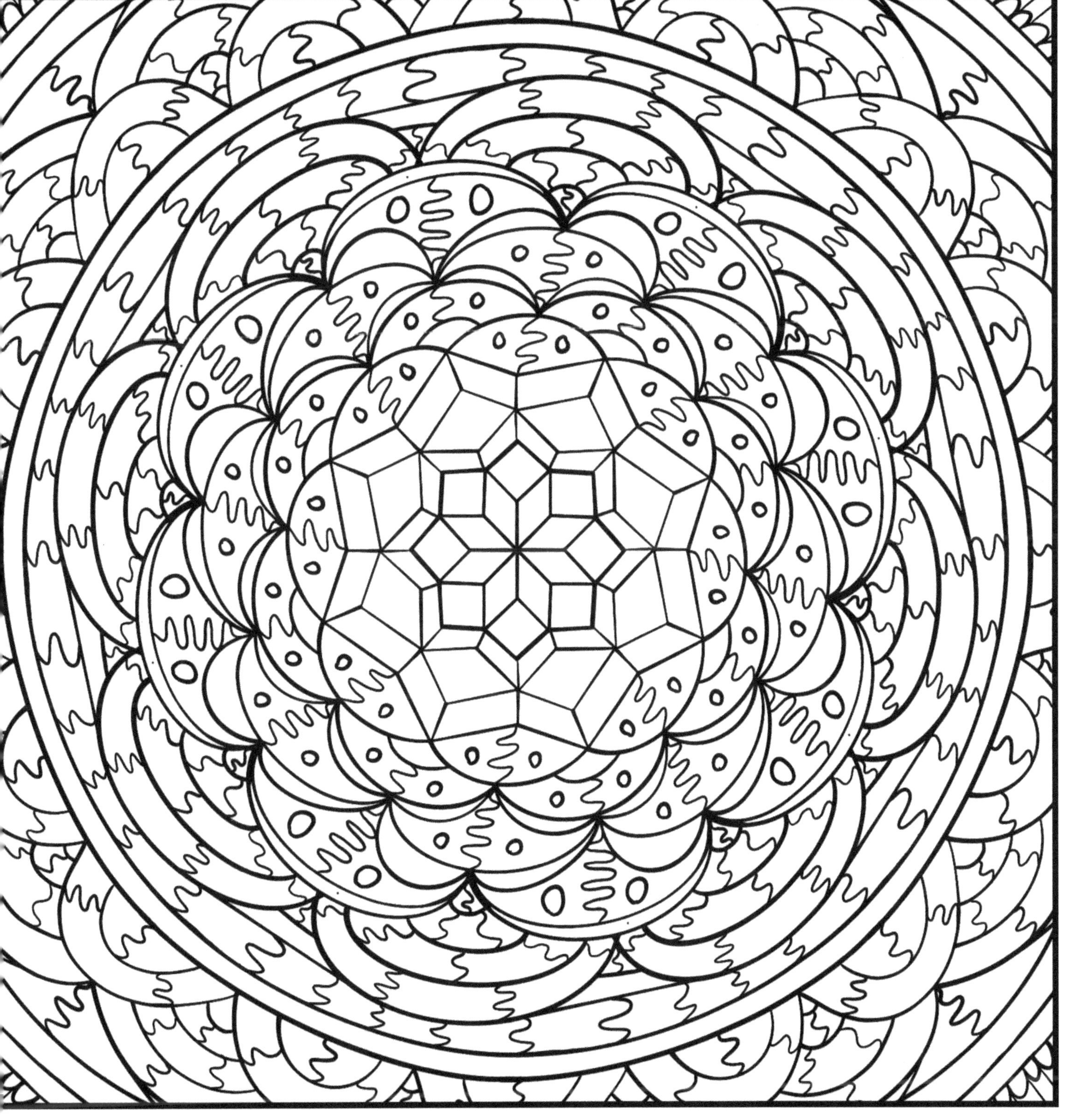

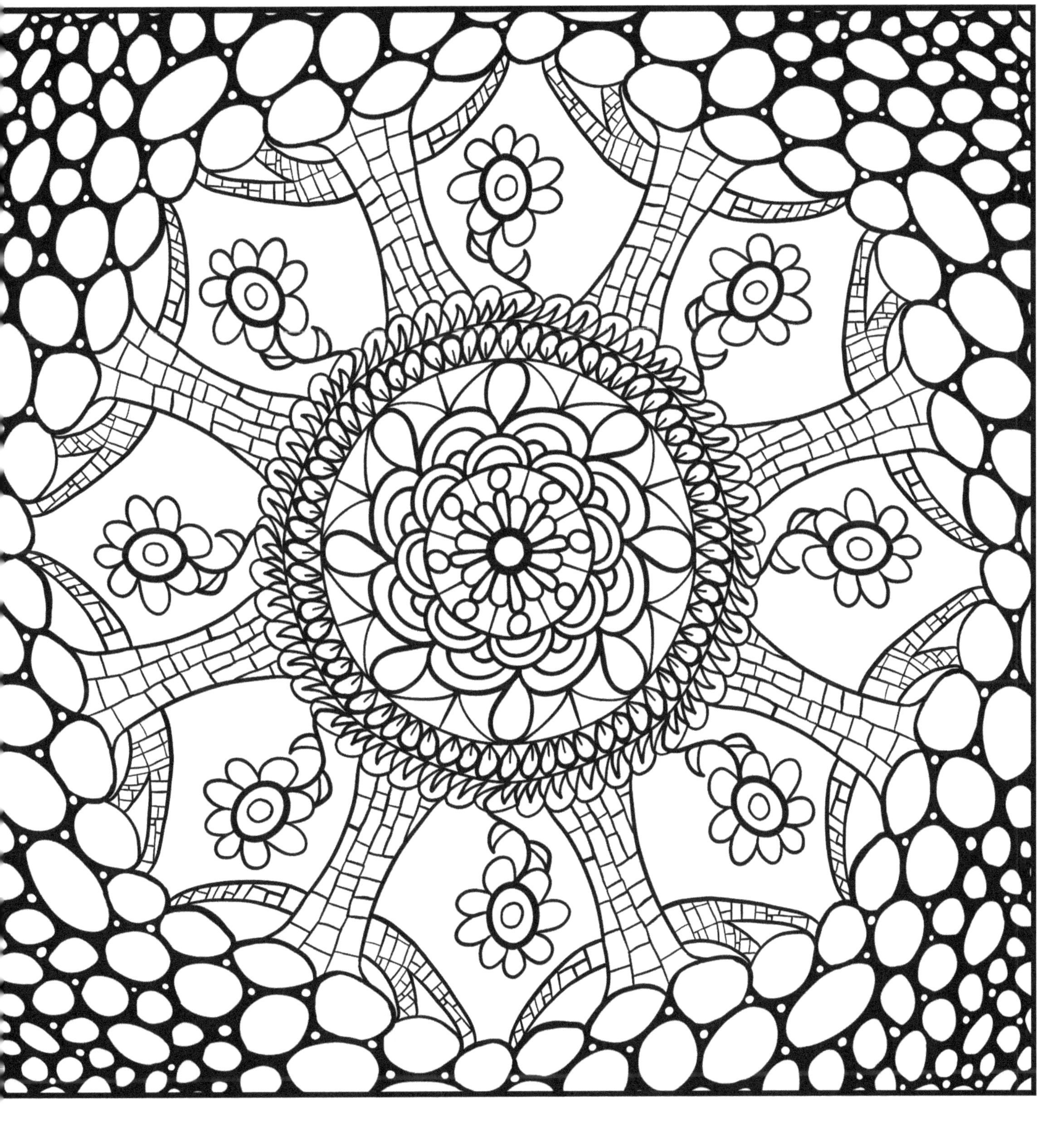

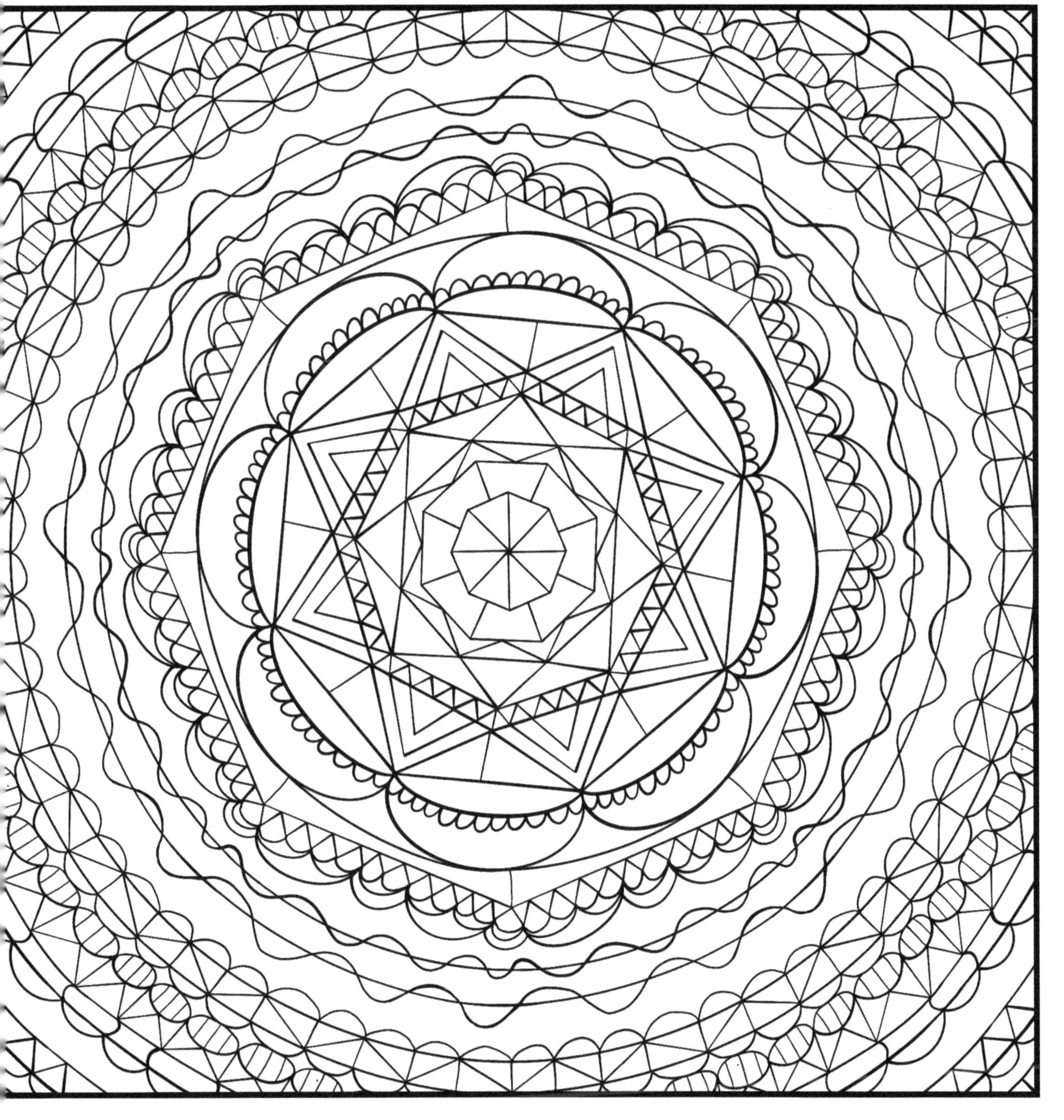

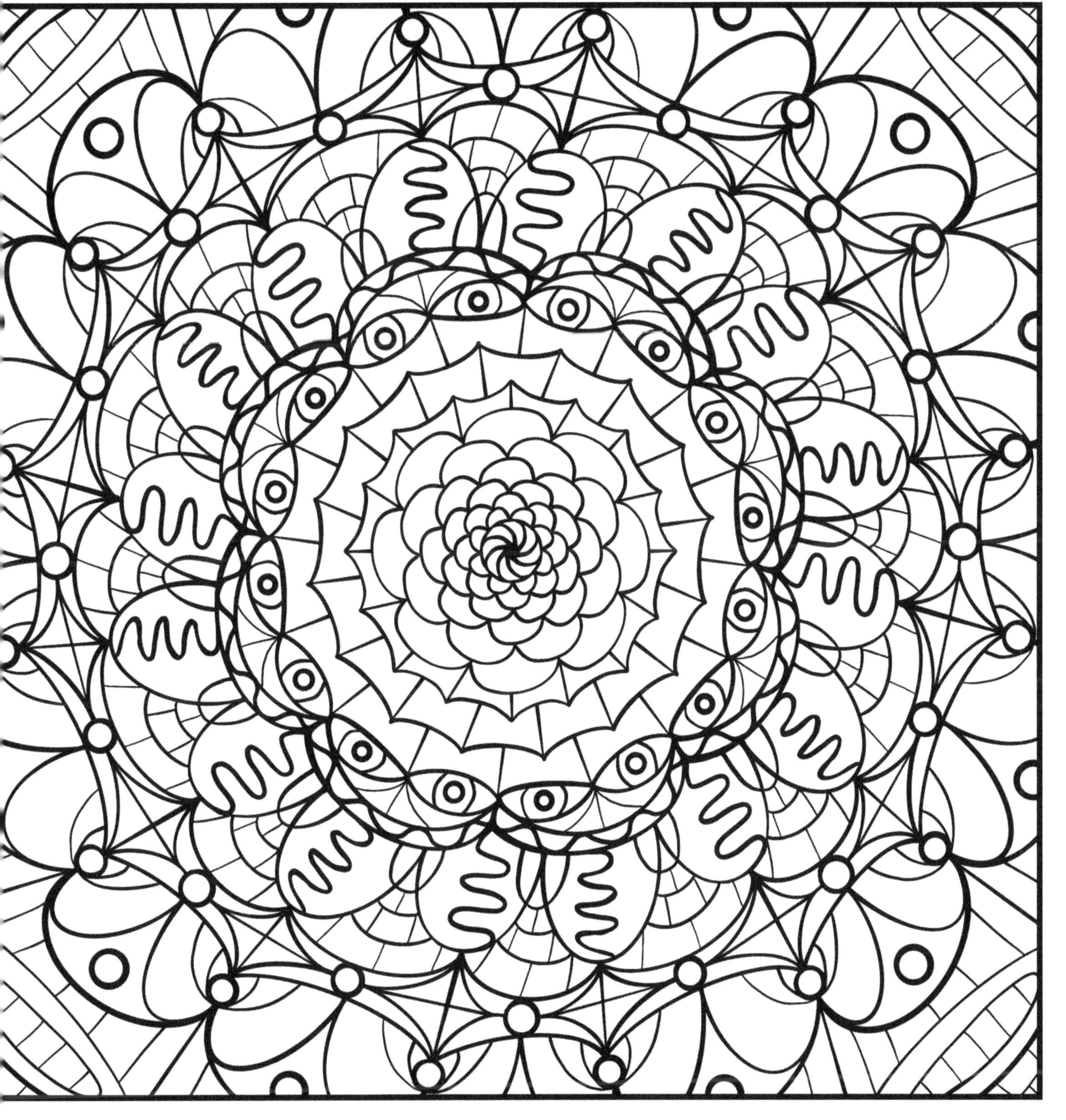

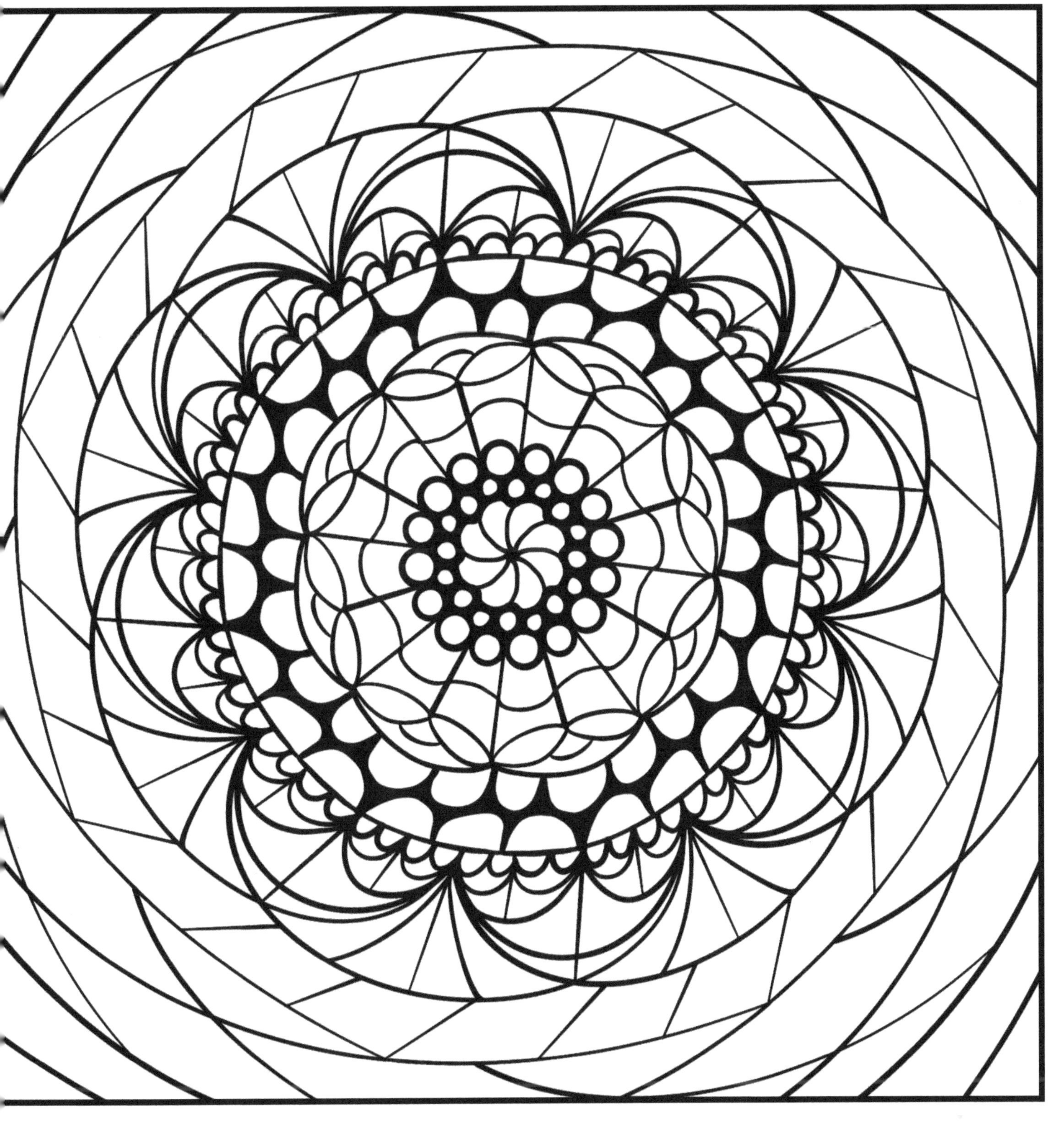

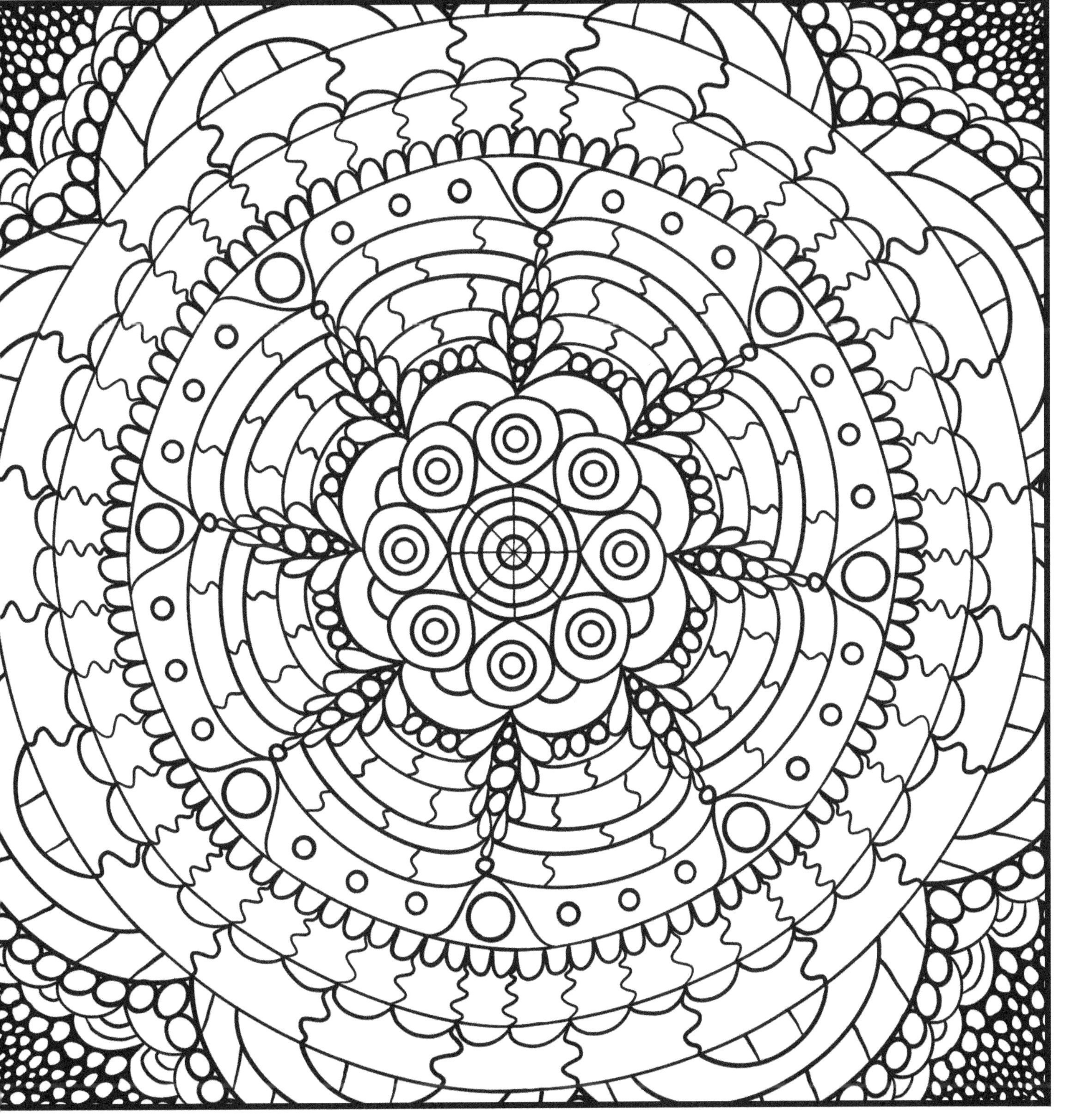

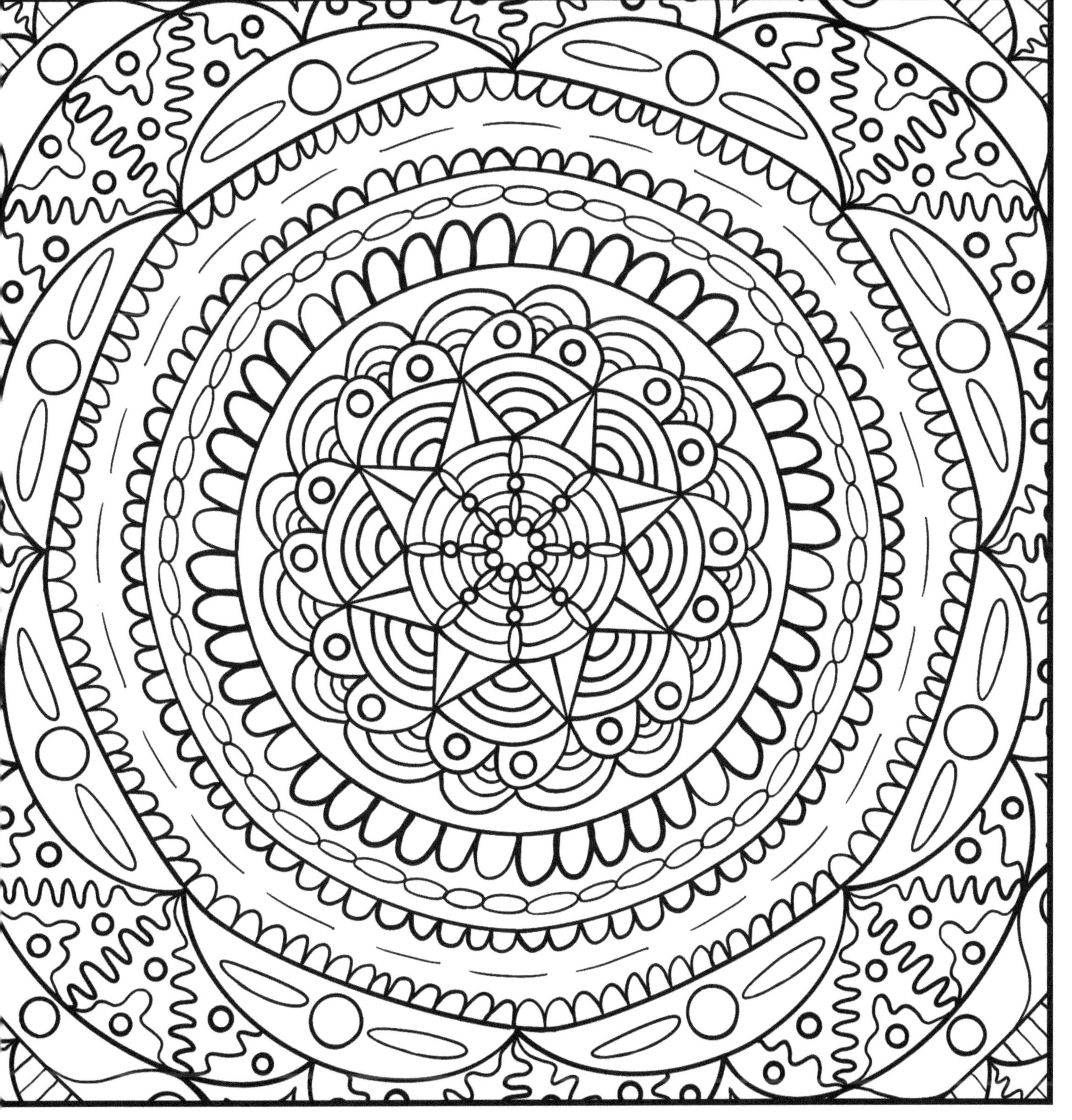

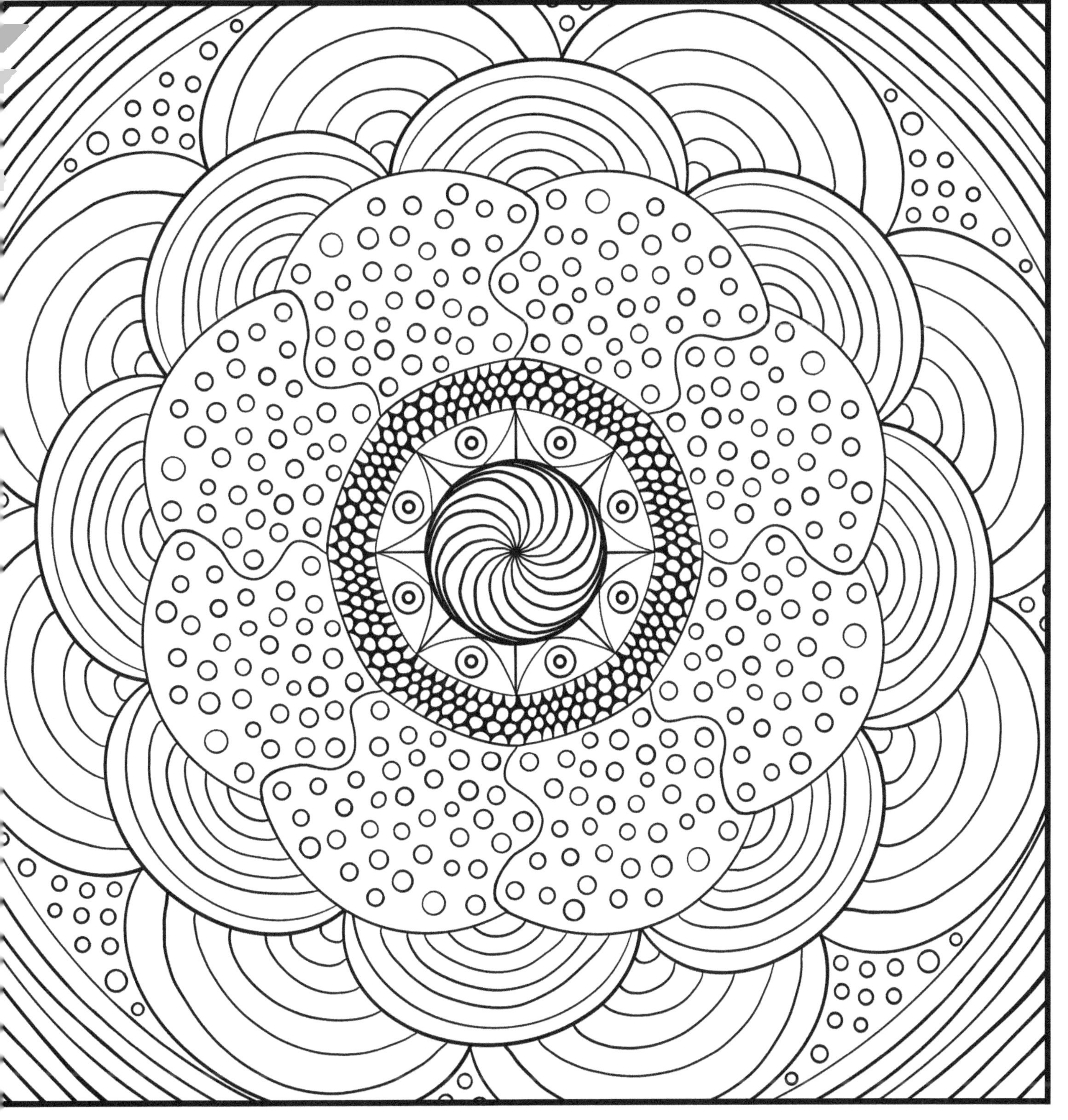

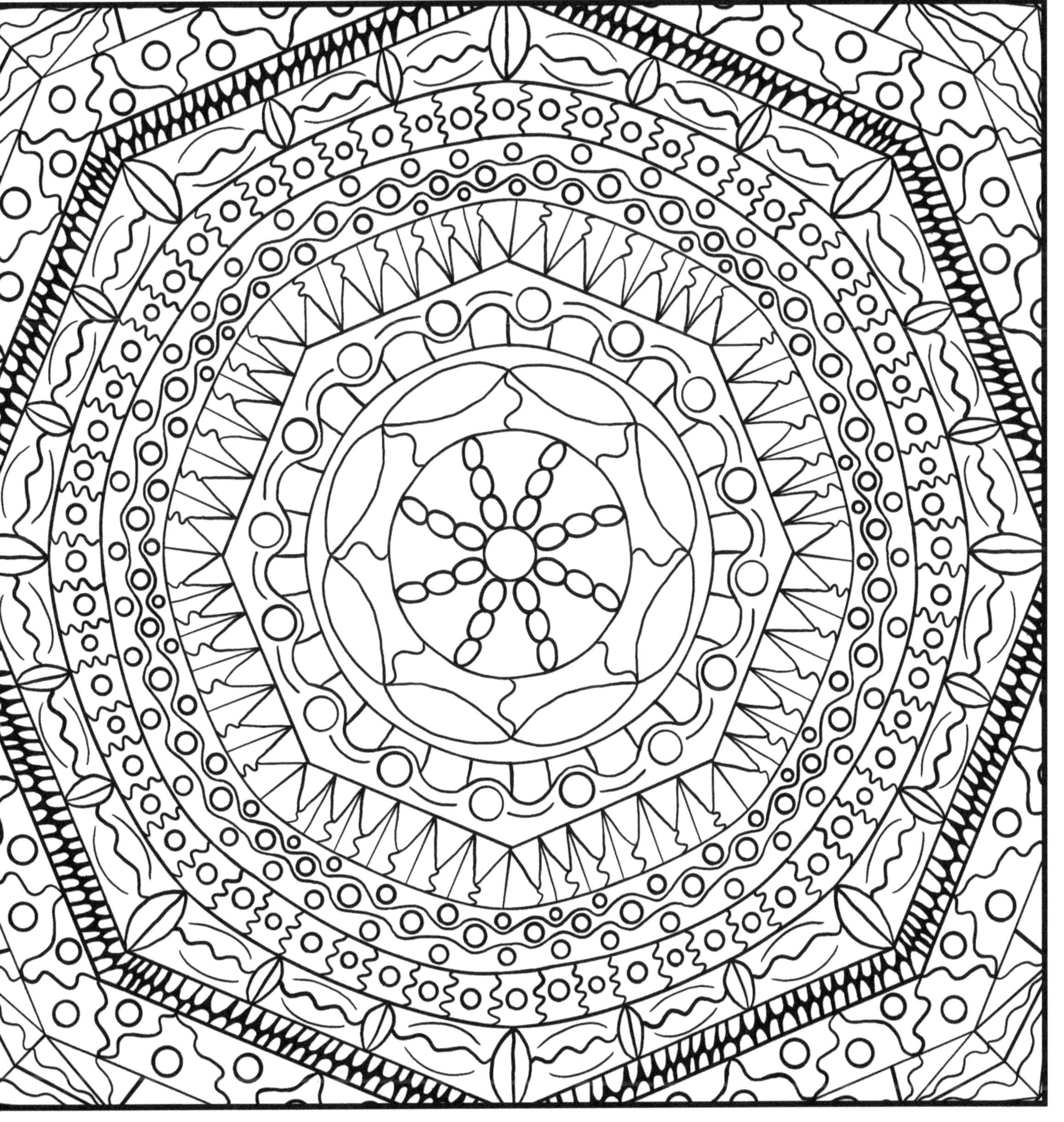

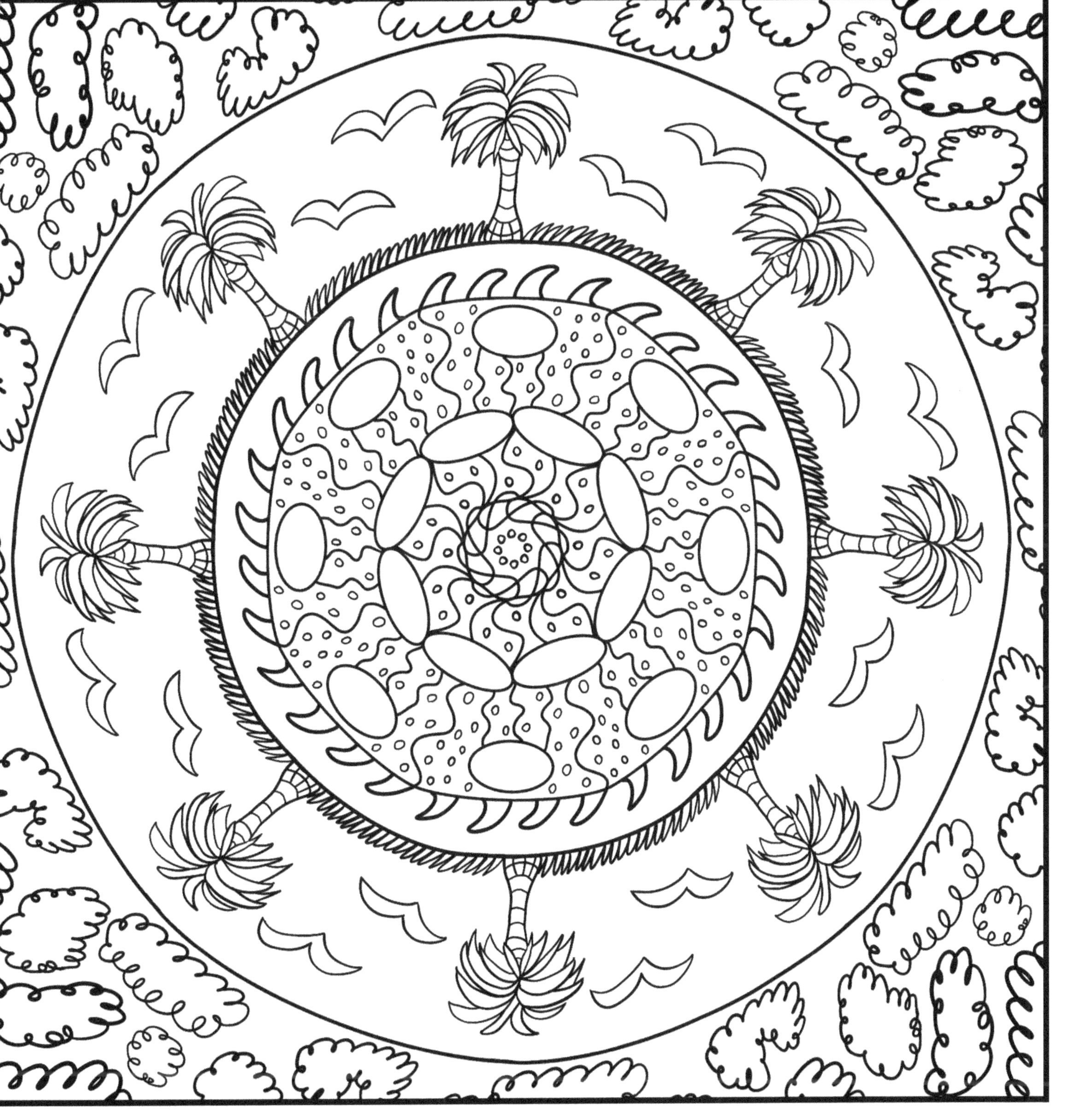

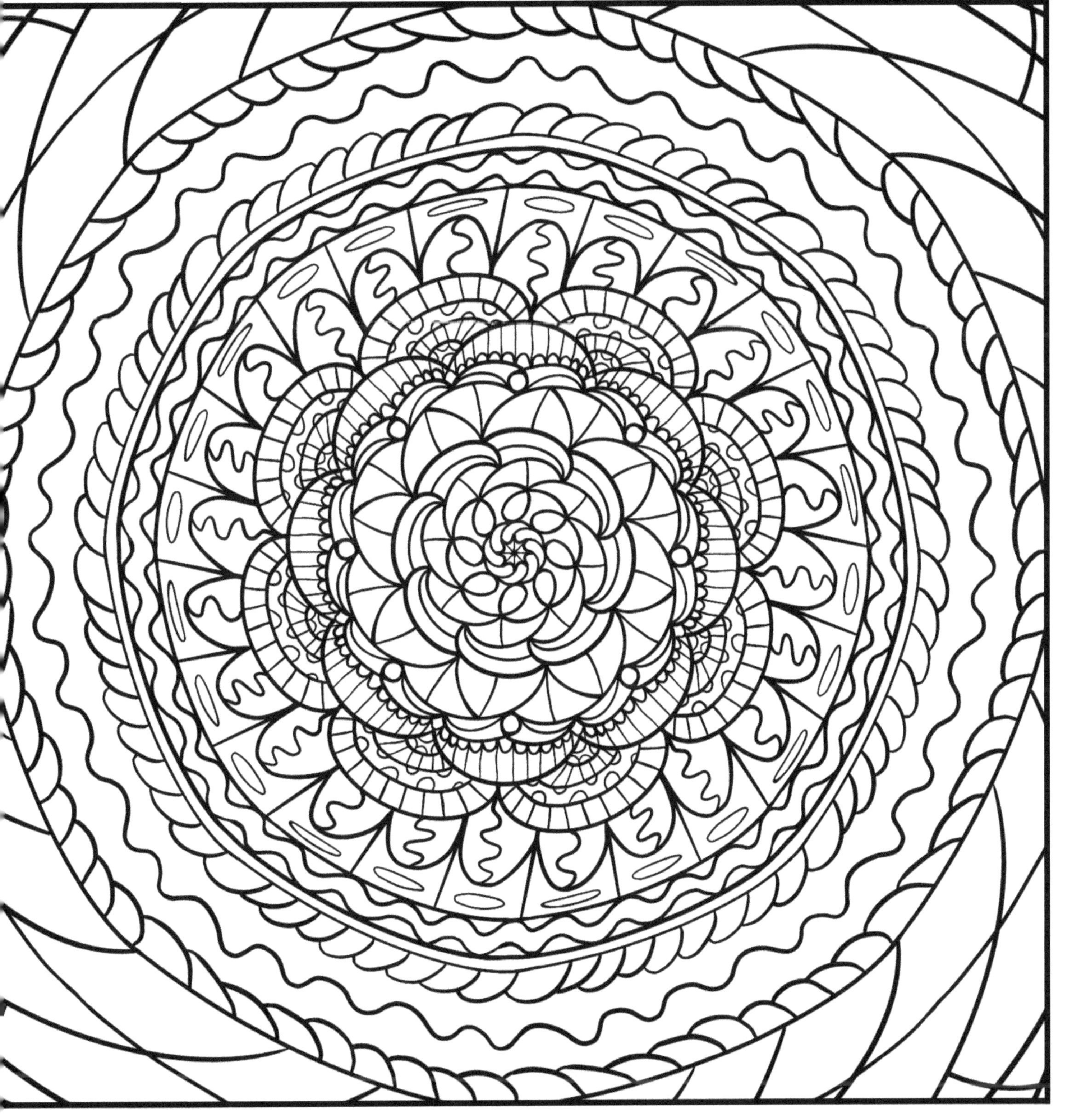

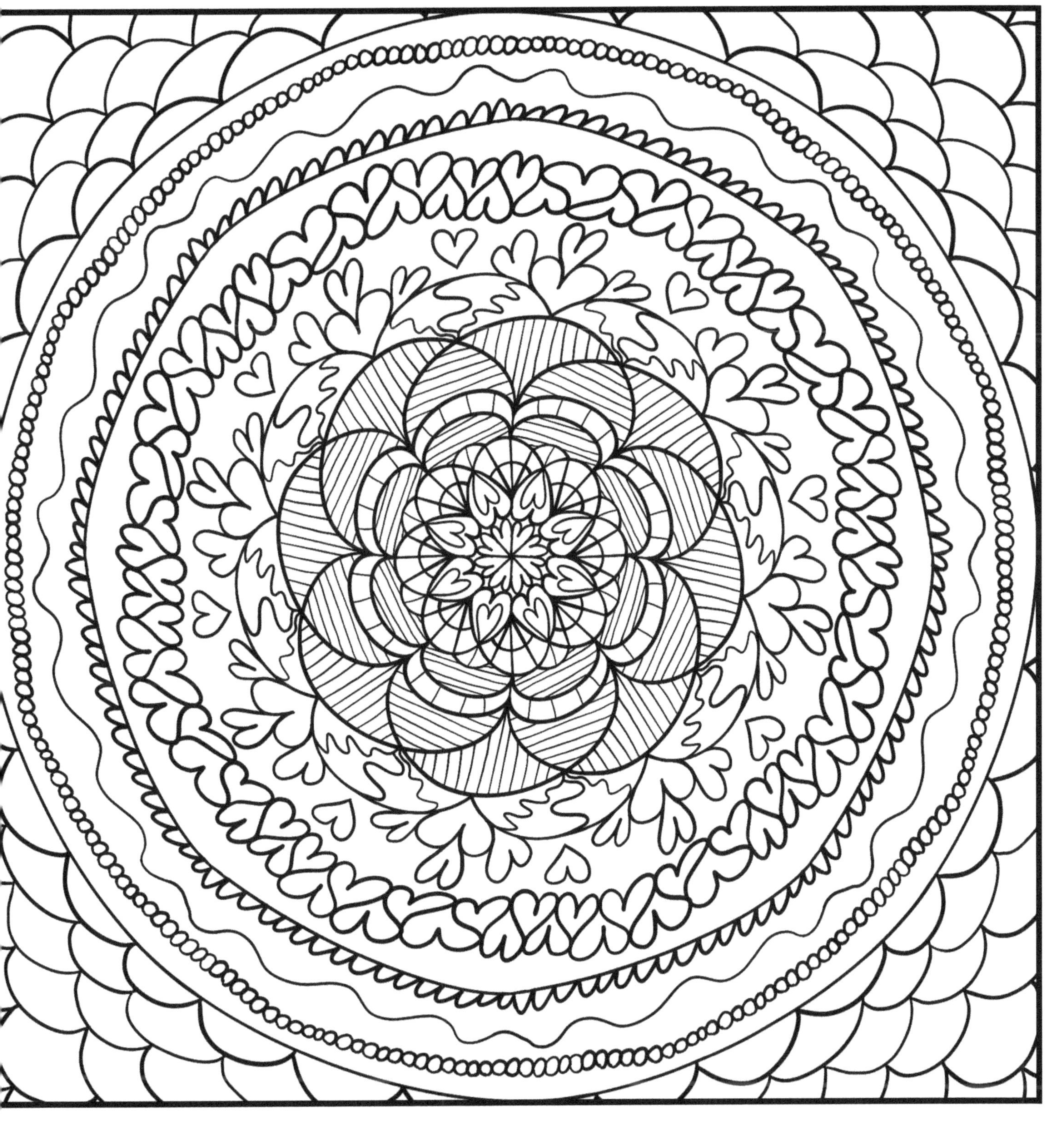

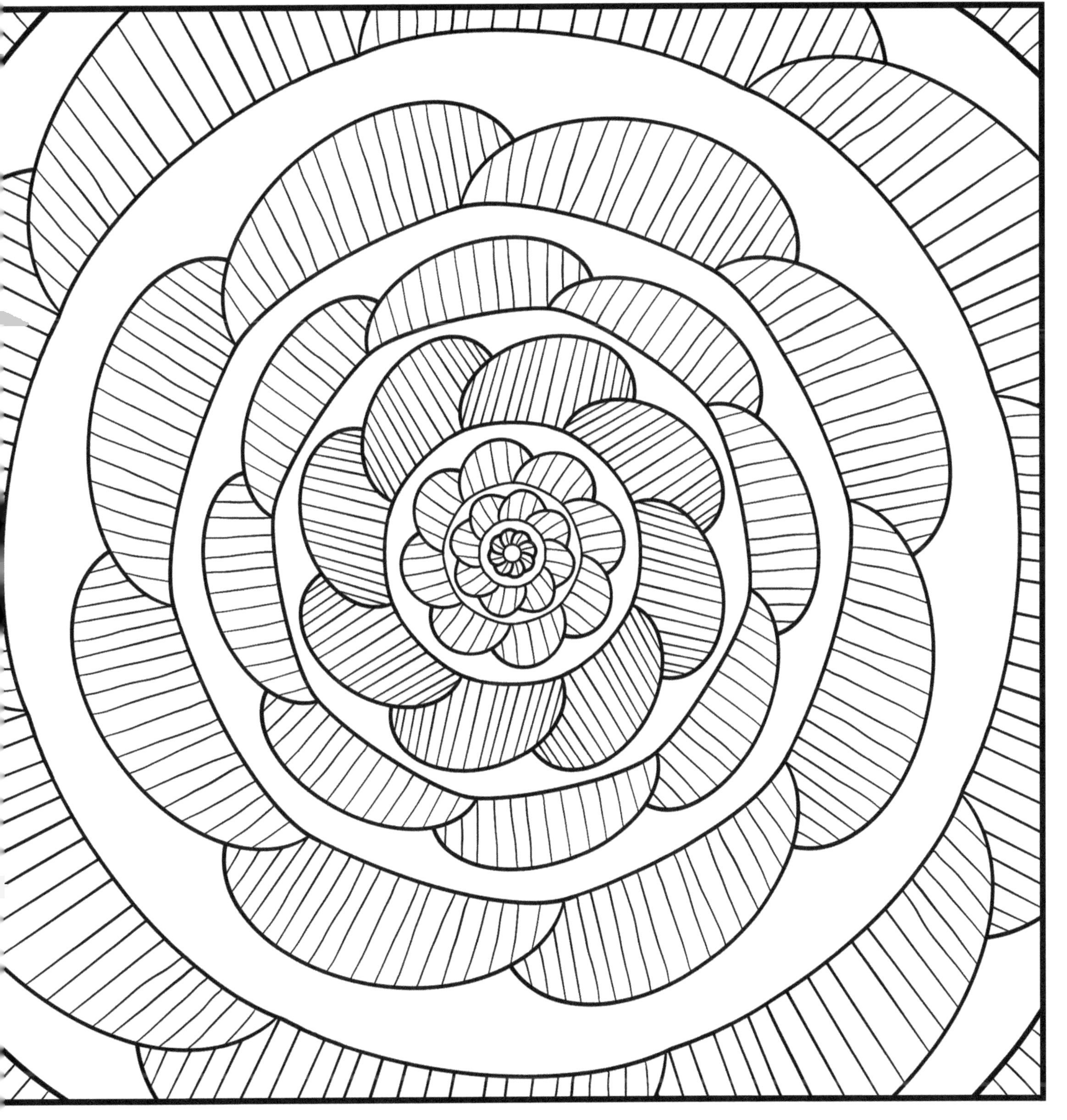

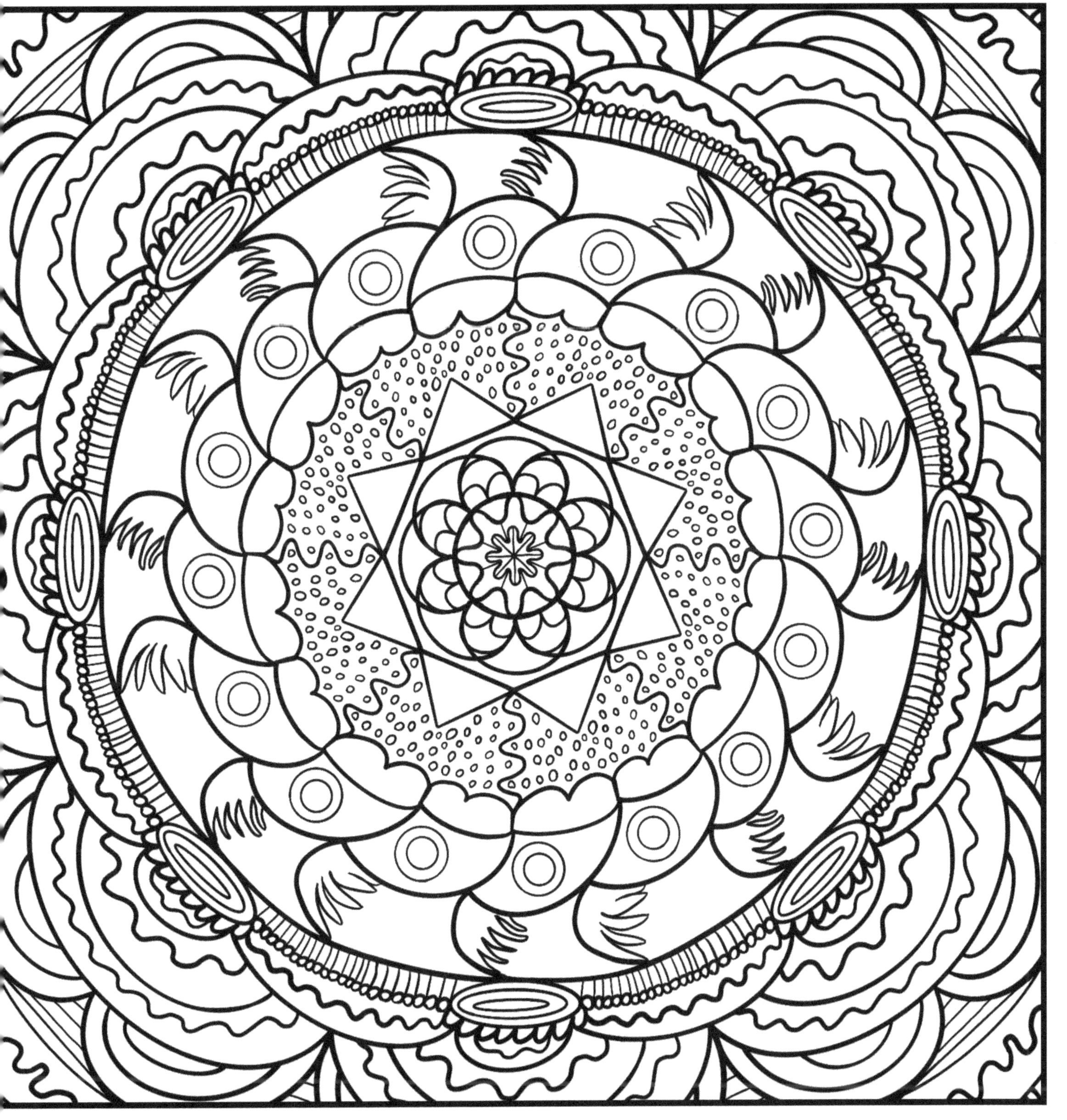

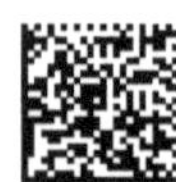
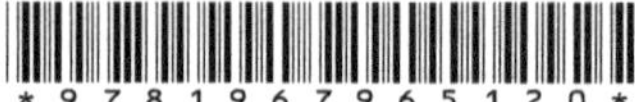